Light

as a

Feather

ISBN: 978-0-9984623-9-4
Swimming with Elephants Publications, LLC

Swimming with Elephants
PUBLICATIONS

Light as a Feather:

an anthology of resilience

Edited by
Courtney A Butler

Introduction

It's time to stop playing it safe.

Even after editing *Light as a Feather, Second Edition*, I still don't want to come clean. I don't want you to know the ugly truth. I want to facilitate educational discussions, support the writers within these pages. Not tell you that I *am* their stories, and they are mine. That if you want to know the truth... just open the damn book.

How can I bear witness to these confessions and not follow through with my own? The very least I can do is be as courageous and as vulnerable as the contributors to this work.

So, here's the truth. I have an eating disorder. It will never go away.

There are days that I am crushed beneath it and my every waking thought is dedicated to obsession. When mirrors distort my reality and I literally, genuinely cannot tell what is real. When I sit in my car weeping alone because I don't know if I am hungry, but I know that I am supposed to eat... but I am too afraid to eat.

There are days when I am livid with a society that convinces me I cannot be beautiful or desirable or valuable unless you can play my exposed ribs like a xylophone, and then have the gall to call me too skinny when I am finally wasting away- all in the same goddamn breath.

There are days when I am inside this disorder so deep, I cannot breathe or think or move, only count. Count the calories. Count the steps. Count the inches of my clothes or the inches around my waist, hips, thighs and chest. Always, always too many inches.

But this is also true- I was finally diagnosed with an eating disorder in 2018. One month later, I was asked to edit this anthology. You can't buy that kind of serendipity! The obsession that plagued me since my first bout of anorexia at 12 years old was given an official name, and soon I began receiving submission after submission from people just like me. Survivors. Their stories became my own, became each other's. Pages bleeding into pages, morphing into a brand-new anthology. My life was starting to transform along with it.

Every single day is a negotiation, but ever so gently, I am finding my way into pockets of peace. Every day I ask my body- *how are you feeling? What would you like to eat? Did you get enough sleep? Do you want to be touched?* My whole life no one ever asked my body what it wanted- especially me. But I am now.

Although it started off shy, I am starting to hear my body speak. Much to my shock, mostly my body is saying thank you. Thank you. Thank you for feeding me, for giving me water, for letting me rest, for taking me out into the sunshine. Thank you for hearing me. For moving me. For taking care of me.

After all this time, my body treasures me in a way that I may never learn to reciprocate. But if I spend the rest of my life trying, it will not be a wasted life.

I am still in the aftermaths of a war, still learning how to lay down arms, but the emotion that inundates me most is gratitude.

Gratitude for my body just as it is, for life and its powerful timing, for this anthology and its writers who brought their souls into this work. Who, unbeknownst to them, inspired me to keep seeking help when all I wanted to do was quit. Who propped me up with their wit and humor and resilience. Who did not give up on themselves, who prioritized their own healing, and inspired me to continue on, telling the radical truth and seeing what happens.

You, dear writers, have my undying gratitude and respect.

I am in awe of you.

~Courtney Butler
Albuquerque, New Mexico
2019

Table of Contents

*Dedicated to all those who have suffered
and survived their own body*

The Ritual.

~Heather Campbell Grimes

I am at a forgettable college party, but the pleasant spring night and porch accessibility make the crowd and the noise tolerable. I sip on cheap beer from the bottle. I am simultaneously flirting with a handful of men, savoring the attention and smoking a cigarette with animated gestures. It is nearing midnight.

Then, the shift. Like a sharp tug on the sleeve. *Set the drink down and come with me*, it says. Obediently, I set down my drink on the railing and drown my unfinished cigarette in its remains.

"I have to go," I say to nobody in particular. And, likely thinking I am simply going to use the bathroom or to fetch another drink, nobody asks.

I make my way down the stairs and climb into my little red Honda, which is parked just out front. The scene of young, beautiful partygoers on the porch and lawn shrinks in the confines of my review mirror.

Once down the block, I turn on my music and roll down the windows; the air pours in like I've spent too long in the deep end. At the stoplight I lay my head out the window and look up at the stars. My mind is empty of its usual toxins—anxiety, discursion, uncertain fear—and I am flooded with a clarity of focus.

White Castle, which is open all night, is where I start. The woman behind the drive-through window has grease-smudged glasses and visible hair on her upper lip. I feel an overwhelming sense of love for her, in spite of her obvious disgust with the situation and, in turn, with me. She takes my money and slinks away from the window to holler at a co-worker as I reach for the bag of fries and onion rings she left on the window shelf.

I allow myself only one bite of each item. The rest must wait until home, until the clock officially begins. I read somewhere that it takes an hour for food to digest beyond purge-ability. So anything I consume longer than an hour before vomiting is permanent and the calories *count*. So I am mindful, especially with more shopping to do before I get home. But a tiny taste reinforces my concentration.

Wendy's across the street has the thicker fries that I am fond of. I'm a little more impatient with this window operator because there is quite a line at the drive-through and he is in absolutely no hurry. Going inside is never an option to me because the face-to-face interaction is a threat to my anonymity. My car fills with the aroma of fried narcotics and I become irritable, suddenly ravenous.

A car full of giggling college girls sits at the speaker in front of me, placing an extensive, disjointed order. Their light beer buzz must have inspired them all to break their respective diets in a collective act of disobedience. That way when they wake up tomorrow and feel like their butts have grown, they can console one-another, reassuring that indeed, their ass is still so sexy.

To complete my list of binge provisions, there is both a Kroger's and a corner-convenience store—large versus small. Kroger's is a sizeable chain grocery store, and I go there for major fixes when I have been blessed with wondrous gaps of free time. It is for the rare occasion when there are no roommates at home, no appointments, an entire afternoon to dedicate to my ritual, a complete evening-into-night to rest and recover. These are the times when I actually *shop*, sometimes from a list, at times even buying an entire birthday cake, telling the baker, "No thanks, I'll just write the name on it when I get home." Then I lie to the cashier about the party I am throwing with all this food.

A smaller convenience store is for most situations, like tonight. It has all the basic necessities to balance the greasy-salty goods with low quality, prepackaged sweets and ice cream. Ice cream is of crucial importance and is only bought in pints, because what is left (if any) will be disposed of at the completion of the evening. In fact, all wrappers and evidence of the ritual are to be thrown away with the purge. Baby. Bathwater.

The cashier at the convenience store next to my apartment knows me. During the daylight hours, being recognized—and the recognition of others—is a thing of great joy. Connection is a thing that comes naturally to me. I take every opportunity to promote those around me out of the status of 'stranger.' I try to remember the names of their family members and ask about their kid's new school or the vacation they took. I linger when possible, listen intently.

But, as I gather necessities for my ritual, there is no time for relationships. When I see someone I know, I am short and rushed. I avoid interaction entirely.

So, I supplement my needs from various gas stations around campus where I am a total unknown, awash in the mass of drunken college students.

In most cases, I don't purchase too much from one place, for someone might consider me indulgent. During the daylight hours, there is no place for a thing as messy and unpredictable as *indulgence.* Daytime is filled with salads and measured low-fat yogurt, platonic relationships and fitted clothing. But once the sun finally sinks beyond the horizon line, we take advantage of the shadowy nooks. We loosen our buckles and pour the alcohol freely. Smoke seeps from noses and mouths like we are on fire.

Then I make my way home to be with my food.

I turn the music off in my car a block away from home. I live alone in an apartment building with two floors, and need to pass the windows of many of my neighbors to get to the staircase and climb to get to my second-story front door. I make myself as invisible as possible, putting all the fast food bags into one grocery-sized bag in case I run into someone on the way. I close the car door gently and am careful to avoid audibly crinkling the bag. I skip stairs yet am conscious not to let my feet clunk. I have my key ready.

*

It's difficult to pinpoint the specific moment in life where it all officially started. I don't remember a time where food, body, and exercise were *not* a conscious struggle. My mother put me on my first diet at age eight— "Thin Kids," it was called. Similarly, I was on Richard Simmons' "Deal-a-Meal" diet in middle school. Exercise was a thing of punishment for an imperfect—overtly flawed and loathsome—body, as well as the main tool to erase calories. By high school my dysfunctional relationship with food matured alongside a heavy load of depression, making it more difficult to use exercise to keep up with my gloomy overeating. So I tried puking.

Before I could drive, I would sneak downstairs after my parents had gone to bed, alert to avoid the squeaky third step. I would gorge on whatever was available—bread, butter, fake maple syrup. My mother was always on a diet, so the house was not stocked with junk foods. When I turned 16 and got my driver's license, the first thing I did to celebrate my freedom was to drive to Dairy Mart and stock up on my own binge foods—the glory! I remember eating ice cream from the carton while I was driving a straight stretch of country road in my Chrysler New Yorker. I felt so independent, so adult in my aloneness, in spite of the chocolate tributaries that ran down my chin and onto my shirt.

The rituals were not as refined then. Inexperienced as I was, I often performed my purging duties while locked in a bathroom. But, there are no stereos in bathrooms to drown out the noise, and you can't be in there for any length of time without suspicion. Trial and error led me to my first rule of thumb: when living with others, never puke in a toilet. It is impossible to get all the bits to flush down. Doubled-up plastic grocery bags are much more effective.

I moved into my first apartment right out of high school with a boyfriend who worked the graveyard shift (a job I strongly advocated for) and was away almost every night. So it was convenient to finish my days with a ritual. I could have gotten away without him ever really knowing had it not been for the irrepressible moods swings.

Next I lived with a roommate whom I encouraged to visit her boyfriend across the street as often as possible. As with my previous boyfriend, I committed to re-stock any of my roommate's food that I had gorged on, regardless of the hour. If I had eaten thirteen of her Oreos before bed, I would force myself to head out into the night in my pajamas to replace them. That way, when the sun came up, everything would be just as it was the day before and all that was consumed in the dark could be forgotten.

The most challenging place to maintain my ritual was when I spent a semester of college in London. I harbored hope that going abroad would break the deeply embedded and masochistic routine I found myself a daily victim to. I lived with a host family and was "lucky" enough to have my own room, something many other students were not privileged with.

But between the family of five and my other American roommate across the hall, it was a rare occasion to have the house alone in the evening. So I tailored my habits to suit the circumstances. I came home between classes, or skipped them entirely when the house was empty, to feast on a selection of foreign goods I'd picked up: cheese-filled pastries from the train station, Cadbury chocolate bars from the vending machines, danishes from the local bakery on the corner. There were also many occasions, especially on weekends, when I would eat for the entire hour-long commute home on the train from a night out. Other travelers came and went, so the only witness to the level of my consumption was the security camera and my own scathing conscience.

Purging was quite difficult in those far-off environs; executed properly only when I was sure that none of the six people I lived with would walk through the door. I wound up substituting the purge by overindulging continuously with no real beginning or end. I was pervaded by discomfort and a low-grade-numbness as I strolled the Tate, took a bus by Trafalgar Square and had brief romantic affairs with our school bus driver and a handful of other students. I also developed an embarrassing habit of getting into the goodies that belonged to my host family's young children after everyone had gone to sleep. (In retrospect, I can't help but wonder if the kids noticed the surplus of their treats—tucked high and away in the cupboard—dwindling away with no explanation.) I returned to the states wearing fifteen extra pounds as my main souvenir.

Each of these situations, with their obstacles to my evening ritual, felt like initiation for the time when I was to finally graduate to a place of my own. So gorgeous is a space where no one will come home unexpectedly and no one will notice if the enchiladas they saved for lunch are gone. No fear of being caught in the act after the binge and before the purge, unwittingly pulling the plug on my duteous program.

*

I am home. With the click of the door behind me, I feel safe and contained. I switch on just enough light to be able to see. I close the curtains and turn on the TV. A feeling of glee bubbles up, like a child about to open gifts. I set it all up as gracefully and meticulously as a shrine. Ice cream (microwaved just a hair in its original container to soften around the edges, never transferred to a bowl), fried stuff spilled on a plate (often microwaved a bit because of the heat lost in the commute), sweets on another plate, (complete segregation of sweet and salty items is a must), and a glass of milk (for extra lubrication when it all comes back up). The plates and food items are lined up on the rug between the television and me, edges aligned. I check the time and begin.

With the first few bites, always ice cream, I feel joy. A palpable and sudden feeling of victory. My jaw and shoulders relax, as if my needs are finally being met, as if this situation is the salve that cures everything that hurts. I eat ice cream throughout the binge to grease the system for the future purge, and also as a mile-marker. I know that later, when the ice-cream stops coming up into the grocery bags, I am done.

Thoughts like *I shouldn't do this* or *I will get fat* or even a pragmatic *WTF am I doing??* are not part of the experience. I am a programmed monkey with skin-walls and robotic arms. I ask no questions. I am unable to recall the hundreds of times I've done this before and the same devastating way it always turns out.

I don't give the TV much attention; it's just company. At

first, the food tastes intoxicatingly delicious. Core-satisfying. I laugh and grin to the empty room. I snuggle into my clothes, feel the comfort in every bone, between every joint. My cat is curled up in a ball on the couch so tightly I cannot see her head. *That* is the feeling.

But that feeling doesn't linger as long as I want it to. That feeling has a hungry, sucking, parasitic mouth and, *goddamit*, it demands I keep feeding it. But I am getting full. The food begins to all taste the same because my taste buds are wilting from abuse. The TV begins to seem abrasive and assaulting. Nausea waves through me if I put down the food for just a moment. It's fifteen minutes in. I wish the good feeling would last longer. I wish it didn't turn ugly so quickly. I am still eating, forcing, stuffing with greater hostility and speed. I'm chewing less so that it will come back up with less effort. I audibly grunt between bites.

Things have skewed. The feeling, that fucker, has turned on me.

The hypnotic exuberance has been replaced by grueling self-loathing and darkness. I am desperate for that euphoria to come back, to show her pretty little head again. I am willing to torture myself for the possibility of laying my eyes on her another time.

I continue consuming, gobbling, vindictively and out of punishment now. It is my fault the elation is gone. I am in this hell realm because I made a collection of shitty choices. Forgoing penalty would be a senseless endorsement for it to happen again tomorrow.

At this tipping point, it is as if a portal opens. I am pounded by a vicious cascade of memories of the countless times I have been here before, in this very moment, in this very situation. Now the thoughts, here the come: *What have I done?* and *Oh jesus, I hate this part* and *Fuck! Not again!*

The last bite is like a bear claw to the abdomen. I take the generously rolled out paper towels and the doubled-up plastic grocery bags (having learned the hard way that one is not enough) and I go into the hallway. A change of scene is essential.

I sit on my knees in execution-position and trigger myself to puke by sliding two fingers down my throat. I am suddenly exhausted and want it all to be over. I want nothing more than to fall asleep in the warm embrace of a loving, knowing person. It takes a few tries to get vomit to start coming up, but once it does it flows somewhat on its own. The ice cream pours out in splatters. I cough in between but don't stop yet to wipe my mouth because pausing screws up the rhythm of the exorcism. I purge until there is nothing left inside me and I am emphatically empty in every way.

I pull myself up in the middle of what appears to be a crime scene. I rinse out my mouth in the sink, having been told that the act of brushing would spread tooth-decaying acids. I gather every bit of evidence—all containers and wrappers right down to a stack of un-used White Castle napkins—into the bags used for purging. It is absolutely not an option to collapse until all the markings of the evening's ritual have been removed in double-knotted bags that feel disproportionately heavy to lift. I head out to the dumpster behind the building.

The chill in the air floods my lungs and keeps me from full and immediate disintegration. I am no longer worried about crossing paths with a neighbor. Quite the opposite. I find myself lingering in front of windows as I walk and taking weighty, slow steps on the stairs.

When I return to my door, I pause to have a look at the row

of neighboring apartments on my floor. There is a fleeting thought to knock on one of the doors, to make a connection.

But all the curtains are drawn, so I go inside.

Heather Campbell Grimes

Heather Campbell Grimes writes to gain perspective on everything from parenting to Alzheimer's disease to eating disorders to relationships. She loves a well-told story of any kind—especially ones that are true. Her essays have appeared in *Mindful*, *Mindful.org*, and *Elephant Journal*. She has also told many of her stories on stage and recently completed a non-fiction children's picture book manuscript about Buddhism.

Heather is a licensed massage therapist who works primarily with seniors who have Alzheimer's disease and dementia. She uses her connection with elders to collect their stories and, when appropriate, she archives their musings on cd, in their own voices. She is also active in the local foster care community. Heather has a special appreciation for alpacas, a well-trimmed hedge, imperfect quilting, and easy guitar songs. She has been free of disordered eating for over ten years and lives with her husband and two young daughters just outside Boulder, Colorado.

She Doesn't Need to See the Menu

~Blythe Baird

I am watching you get sick.

The whites of your eyes
are becoming yellow yolks.
Cheeks hang like grocery bags.

You make diets of day planners.
No time to eat with a stuffed calendar.

Meals are powdered hot chocolate packets.
Breakfast is tap water. NyQuil: a midnight snack.

To invite happiness inside him,
Vincent Van Gogh drank paint of yellow hues.
You do mad things for happiness, too.

Vomit for an after school sport.
Your teeth blister.

Bathe in sea salt to dehydrate
water weight.

Eating disorders are very in.
Like kale, like skinny jeans, like old
Hollywood glamour- and don't you dare
bring up Marilyn Monroe.

Recent studies show her frame was only
one third of what you think.

Shrivel your stomach until it takes a single
granola bar to feel full. With pale pupils and
unplugged irises, the only language
you communicate in is numbers.

You are a human recycling bin.
Blame your hometown, your mother,
anything but your skin.

If you are not recovering,
you are dying.

There was another girl in our grade who got
sick about the same time you did, but she went
to the hospital real quick,

Because she was already thin to begin with.
You were not thin to begin with.

You were fat, and now you're evaporating,
so everybody is congratulating you
on getting "healthy."

You are not an illness, but an inspiration.
Your father still carries your before-and-after photo
in his wallet. Your disease is a smashing sensation.

Friend, I am so sorry. You too, are sick.
Your messiah Kate Moss insists,
"Nothing tastes as good as skinny feels."

Girl, she's never had Nutella. Do not trust her,
her two-faced dental care, or her fur pelt.

Anorexics develop hair all over to thaw their glacial
bodies, called lanugo. The cold will not let you go.

Veins bulging like a pop up book,
I am watching you get sick.

Mistake tracing paper for your skin.
I am watching you get sick.

When the blackouts start and your pulse gets
slippery, wallpaper your interior with laxatives.
I am watching you get sick.

Read so much, your body trusts it is
full on authors, not high on hunger.
I am watching you get sick.

One day, you will learn.

The natural pigments will return-
no more yellow skin, no blue fingernails,
no red scratch in your throat matching the
nick on your middle finger.
Make amends with the kitchen.
Your face will glow like a television.
You will get full again. Be able to finish a meal.

One day, I hope I'll be able to finish this poem and say-

I am watching you heal.
I am watching you get better.

Blyth Baird

Originally from the northwest suburbs of Chicago, the viral and award-winning writer has garnered international recognition for her poems that speak out on sexual assault, mental illness, eating disorder recovery, sexuality, and healing.

Her work has been featured by Glamour, TedxMinneapolis, The National Eating Disorder Association, Mic, The Huffington Post, EverydayFeminism, VICE, The Mighty, The Body Is Not An Apology, Write Bloody, Button Poetry, A-Plus, and more.

Eat the Fucking Cookie

~Laura Burgess

It started when I was 10.

It was summer and I was walking on the newly laid tarmac to my friends house across the street. I noticed my thighs rubbed together and that bothered me more than my bare feet getting blistered.

There was no internet then. All I had access to were ridiculous ads in magazines my mom brought home.

"The grapefruit diet!"

"Beach Body in 6 weeks!"

"Miracle fat cure!"

I was a kid with no guidance and my mother was...not a role model in any aspect.

I didn't believe in a lot, I just knew I refused to be like her.
At all. And that meant being thin.

By 13 I was stealing laxatives from Walgreens and forcing myself to puke if I ate something other than oranges, egg whites, or lettuce.
I'd start a binge with eating a carrot, because when that finally came back up in the toilet I knew I had 'got it all out'.

Years filled of foster homes, juvie, sexual abuse.

Running away.

Rinse and repeat.

I felt guilty not only for eating, but for also eating other people's meals, even though the system cut them a check. I learned the only safety I found was in control. And at 16 the only control I had was in my relationship with food. My body didn't belong to me. Not in my head and definitely not in the area of consent or where the state placed me that month. My comfort in having the illusion of actually dictating events in my life followed my plate and mirror and protein smoothie and porcelain confidant.

I was pretty good at hiding it.

I found other outlets in my 20s.

That tough girl facade.

Yeah. I was that bad ass mountain biking, snowboarding, show the boys up bitch with a phony attitude.

I was into fitness, right?

I was addicted to adrenaline and ego, it truly had nothing to do with that scale and the way my clothes fit, right?

I was not on a diet, I was training!

I stopped purging, broke up with my toilet face time and thought I fucking won!

Life went on and just because I wasn't regurgitating nutrients meant I was ok.

Right?

Yet, I weighed myself three times a day. I calculated my calories and exercised to the point of a complimentary image.

But. I continued to feel empty and I tried to fill that hole with men and women. Men and women and new shiny things. Things that left me starving.

Still. Years. Recipes. Running shoes. Blue ribbons. Medals. Identity.

Size 2.

Then I got pregnant.

On purpose.

I mean I was a new nurse and had my life together. I always wanted a real family. It was the next thing to conquer, and I had become a warrior.

I remember at the halfway mark of my pregnancy I had increased by only 3 pounds. Not 20 as recommended. I slathered my stomach in so much cocoa butter my shirts and scrub tops had oily stains. Like a bull's-eye.

My body and sense of control was more important than cravings and realistic gain. The baby was growing and developing fine, leave me alone.

I did put on enough weight the last trimester to not only birth a healthy daughter, but also rebirth my disorder in it's antiquated form.

"You look great for just having a baby!" was actually congratulating my disease. Reinforcing my need to fit into a shape prescribed by an invisible club I'd never be welcomed. That club in my head. Eternal outsider.

I scaled motherhood and stuffed unneeded worries about stretch marks and extra skin with fitting back into my $200 jeans. With the fancy stroller and my baby as a weight in mommy yoga classes.

And many visits to the bathroom.

I yoyo'd with size and depression. With identity and social expectations. I was terrified of anyone really seeing me. I surely couldn't, I had no clue who the hell I was and I wore everyday like a costume for an audition to a part I knew I couldn't pull off. I felt miscast for my life.

Watching my daughter toddle in to attempt to hold my hair as I divorced my lunch was the kick in the gut I needed. How the hell could I teach this human that I loved, more than I knew I ever could, to be strong and proud and feel about herself the way I feel for her? How could I protect her from this shitty world that already has a hand up on her? I realized I, too, was not a role model and I refused to infect her with my defective thoughts. I wanted her to be happy. Fat, skinny, ugly, pretty, it didn't matter. She mattered.

I threw my scale away. I bought stretchy pants and skirts. I cried.

A lot.

I relapsed in secret many, many times, but eventually I just...moved on.

I got busy.

I played with her and read to her and became obsessed with

discovering empowering stories and educational toys. With growing a garden.

Watching her pluck fresh tomatoes off the vine to eat is a healing vision I will cherish forever. I managed to continue a positive affair with food and exercise, despite leaving her father.

Sometimes people only love the sick version of you.

I remember the day last summer I saw her list of goals hanging on her wall :
-   Spend more time with family
-   Exercise more
-   Eat healthier
-   Lose some weight

It broke me a little. Destroyed me actually. She was 12. And gorgeous and developing and nowhere near overweight. She has my same small frame, strong and compact.

"At least she put three things before her self image," my therapist reminded.

I didn't discuss it with her, I just offered to let her cook more, to pick seeds for the garden, to go on walks and bike rides more, and reminded her how proud I am of her daily.

See, I thought she was fine.

And she probably is. She can do her makeup, in 7th grade, better than a Sephora consultant, but doesn't need to wear it everyday, or to shave her armpits, or follow trends.

"I really don't care, mom"

I want to be her when I grow up.

The irony is I've been struggling with some major health issues lately. Chemo will kill the cancer but it can rob your sense of smell and taste. For months everything was wet cardboard mush in my mouth For months I had to make amends with my abusive ex: vomit.

It also destroyed my Vagal nerve. Paralyzed my stomach.
I can finally taste food and smell it again. It's glorious. Delicious. Pleasure I forgot was so wonderful, wrapped in guilt for not cherishing it most of my life.

But I can't keep much down.

If Karma is truth, I got my serving.

Eighteen months to five years to heal nerve damage is what I've read.

Been told.

Instead of researching exercises and low carb menus, I consume medical journals. I devour cookbooks. I cry into pots of sustenance that I can't enjoy.

Healing over the years meant food turned into a way for me to tell my friends, family, and children "I love you." And to tell myself that also.

Now, love is making a dinner I can't eat.

Now, my stretchy pants sag and my legs are boney.

I'd give anything to have my self-perceived 'fat ass' back. To eat a plate of food with jolly company. To feel full and be content with that.

It's sorta comical that years ago, as I actually emotionally repaired, I adopted a phrase.

"Life is short, tomorrow isn't a promise to nobody. Fall in love as often as you can. Spend the money on the good shoes. Allow yourself to laugh, a lot. Eat the fucking cookie. You could get hit by a stray bullet on the way home."

My heart is overflowing, but this time I am maybe starving to death, against my will. Outside of my control.

Laura Burgess

Laura is a mother, philanthropist, advocate, nurse. A writer, seamstress, artist, Jill of all trades and she is madly in love with ABQ. She landed up here as a runaway at 18. Her work can be found in bellies of homeless, open mics, and messy journals.

Finally

~*Sadof Alexander*

My body asked
"will you call me
by the right name?"

So I unlearned
the image of it, shed
thoughts instead of

pounds, hammered
into myself the belief
that this body was

Whole, and not
too much. Often,
I still look at it wrong.

But I call it
by kinder, truer names.
In return, it granted me

permission to finally
demand that I be
called by my own.

Sadof Alexander

Sadof Alexander is an Afghan-American writer. They write highly personal poetry and is always in the slow process of getting better at it.

It's never enough

~Aja-Drew

The number gets
    L
        O
           W
              E
                  R
Mind   d e c a y   i   g

Memories slipping
    Through the cracks in my hands
        Hope falling
    From my fingers, fingertips, and the palms of my hands
Joy drowning
    In the rivers my lungs create

    Too full
    I am too full of holes that even words cannot move without
falling from Heaven and I begin to sink underneath the soil, the soul

Not full enough

    Hungry.
  Never   satisfied.
Mouth waters, forbidden desires,
Food you CANNOT touch, CANNOT eat, CANNOT bathe in,
CANNOT breathe in, CANNOT think about, CANNOT dream about.

Unforgiven.
The frailty of a nightmare.
A spoonful's poison.
The purity that comes with

R
E
S
T
R
I
C
T
I
O
N

...

Push   away   the   plate
Stomach G   R   O   W   L   I   N   G
Heart *pounding*
Heart *slowing*
Heart *stopping*

Only a shell, an empty vase left behind, covered in dust, never used
Nothing but headaches and migraines left   over

I am the prey melting, shivering below
And
I am the black shadow of darkness standing, simmering above.

Aja-Drew

Aja-Drew is a young poet, student, lover of self-expression and all things involving the arts. She is an animal lover, activist, and a world-traveler, who enjoys exploring new cultures and new languages. Aja-Drew is an introverted, shy girl – with a hidden, inner strength, that bursts out of her shell when it is most needed. Using abstract symbolism to form the walls and foundation of her poetry, writing is the best time when she can truly transform into herself and speak her heart's song. She also enjoys learning and teaching; and her poetry is a way she can explore her own vulnerability to rediscover hope when in her darkest moments. She is two years in recovery for Anorexia Nervosa, and tries to see the positive and light in every situation.

A Circular Circus of Crisis and Catharsis

~bassam

You'd thought that you'd hid wanting to die so well, that no one had any idea.

You have thought about death every day of your life, while living a life you were unable to control.

Ever since you were young, you were always afraid of other people. Your parents were angry and abusive, to you and to each other, and so you grew up thinking everyone was only ever going to be angry with you.

However, whenever you'd eat, that fear went away.

And you just kept getting afraid, so you'd keep eating.

Food was the only thing that made you take your mind off your fears, but you weren't actually facing them as you should have; you just kept escaping.

And so you began purging the food after eating it, because you wanted to be able to face those fears.

You binged on the happiness and purged it instead of digesting it, receiving its nutrients, and allowing yourself to continue living.

You also wanted to be thin, and felt you *needed* to be thin.

You felt as if you were destined to become like the ones who used to tease you about your body size, who excluded you because you were different.

The ones who cast you out because you couldn't fit in. Your fat body was told by everyone around it that it did not deserve to exist, and never stopped looking for any way not to.

You'd felt that at some point, you deserved thinness, what you believed to be karma's greatest gift to the universe. It was your religion. You valued and worshipped it.

You would spend 10% of your day and 90% of your energy at the gym, as well as 10% of your salary on diet pills and other supplements. You would also spend hundreds of dollars a month on food you only end up flushing down the drain. Relationships with romantic partners never lasted; you learned that love could be binged on, and purged, too.

Your poisoned mind did everything its power to destroy your own body, break your own heart, and not heal your own soul.

You began writing poetry.

It became your last attempt to document your entire life, by spending your entire life writing about it. That, too, eventually became your entire life, kept in perpetual death through your words.

You use it to hide your own body between lines of stanzas like rows of headstones, and pages of books like crypts and mausoleums.

It is the formaldehyde ink in this corpse of a pen, not to be published, but to embalm. It achieves the death you claim to wish you could bring yourself to. It is far more beautiful and significant than the remains you will leave as a mark on this existence, just in case you never learn to love yourself enough to feel like you deserve a burial.

Except that it wasn't enough: you yearned and craved for congregation and ceremony.

You began performing your poetry in front of audiences.

You never really found love on a stage. You were simply fascinated with how many people were interested in gathering at funerals and watching someone on stage recite their own eulogy, despite being unwilling and/or unable to do anything about it.

They merely bore witness to your told tragedies, and remained silent. They listened, mesmerized, but clapped when it was over.

As if we were pretending to be human, so we could face the fears we have of each other.

You once believed that you were facing those fears by performing poetry. However, it was merely your way to fuel your addiction to fear and food, giving you both something to binge when you became too afraid of the people around, and something to purge when you wanted to face them.

You felt as if you'd reduced yourself to a circus animal in the middle of the ring, embarrassing itself, like Jumbo: the African bush elephant born in 19th century Sudan in that the Disney movie *Dumbo* was actually based on.

What they don't tell you was that, as an infant, he was with his mother when she was killed by hunters.

What they don't tell you was how malnourished he was from being forced to eat coins and drink whiskey.

What they don't tell you was that Jumbo would throw fits of violent rage at night and engage in self harm, having gone as far as smashing his own tusks.

While you were afraid of everyone else being angry with you, your own anger was building inside you.

You let it in through trying to connect with people, and binging food. You let it out through poetry, performance, and purging.

They became your pink elephant hallucinations, followed by periods of deep isolation.

It was a constant cycle of anger and fear, spiraling downward, furiously, and unable to stop, like the flushed toilet bowl that carried your darkness away and made room for more.

You have thought about death every day of your life, while living a life you were unable to control.

You'd thought that you'd hid wanting to die so well, that no one had any idea.

Until you'd finally stopped trying to hide, and told people.

And they actually listen.
And they save your life.

And they are poets, just like you.

Sure, you're afraid of them, but they're also afraid of you and, more surprisingly, each other.

But they would face their collective fears together, and whenever they recognized the other people they're afraid of, they face those fears.

Because you're all part of the same circus.

And while their fear and anger are fuelled through different things, you share the same catharsis: poetry and performance.

Because even though they clapped when it was over, they only did so because they were proud that you were ridding yourself of the pain and trauma you'd been carrying your whole life, by telling your story.

More importantly, they listened while you it was happening.

It was the fear that made you purge the happiness you binged on instead of digesting it and allowing yourself to love yourself enough to feel like you deserve a burial. However, despite the fear, feeling and existing in the moment with others is something far more beautiful and significant than either the body or the words you leave behind.

You were both seen and heard, and while the fear will always be there, so will the love.

Because, just like Jumbo had survived a life of physical pain and emotional trauma, it would still take a train to kill him.

The Recipe

~bassam

In a pan about as shallow as grade-school classmates,
Pat childhood memories dry with tissues and season with poverty.
roast, covered in guilt and self-loathing,
in the middle of a hell-hot playground for 15 minutes,
or until the emotional thermometer registers for depression
Cover with a cold heart for about 10 years.
Measure ingredients by weight, and always use judgement.

Thinly slice verbal abuse and, in a heavy skillet, cook
in clothes that won't fit, with
fat jokes, embarrassment, loneliness and resentment,
stirring until self-esteem is slightly fragile.

Transfer verbal abuse mixture to
another school, lightly beat the most overweight kid in class
with laughter until weakened.
Never use the with-them laughter, only laughter labeled "at-them".
Cut into similar shapes and discard any that differ from the norm,
Preheat brain to 420°F and insert for nine more years.

On a separate, cocaine-dusted mirror on a coffee table,
Form and cut inch-long white lines as desired,
Stir in 1 cup guilt and shame, bake on high for 20-30 minutes.
Blend caffeine, diet pills, and salted sweat;
starve until reduction is evident, for 7-8 months.

Insert verbal abuse mixture with caffeine,
clutch belly, and fold extra skin in a mirror.
Add judgment and bring to a steaming boil.
Letting any ingredients roll of your back at the

others' recommendation ruins the entire recipe at this point.
Keep warm while transferring from counselling to psychotherapy.
roll on a treadmill until drenched in sweat and heart rate reads 160,
for 60 minutes.

Add all ingredients to chilled childhood memories
and a litre of soda, preferably diet, swallow until full.
In a separate lavatory,
(can be public but at home works best for privacy),
turn on cold water faucets, kneel, insert two fingers in mouth.
heaving with abdomen,
purge meal from stomach into bowl.
Repeat until belly flattens.
Repeat until belly flattens.
Repeat until belly flattens.
Repeat until belly looks slimmer.
Repeat until belly is empty.

Flush.
May cause dizziness,
and stomach acid to wear down tooth enamel.
Blood-shot eyes and head rush are temporary;
they'll fade after leaving the restroom.
Garnish with mint to hide the smell of vomit.

Serves none.

bassam

bassam (they/them or xe/xim) is a national poetry slam-winning spoken word artist, proud auntie, and settler currently residing on the unceded Coast Salish territory (of the Musqueam, Squamish, and Tsleil-Waututh First Nations peoples, colonially known as "Vancouver, Canada").

they are a member of the League of Canadian Poets who is currently serving as National Director for Spoken Word Canada, and have performed poetry across Turtle Island.

Little Sister

~Vienna Claire Jeffery

Nine pounds eight ounces. Baby fat and punctual. Doesn't cry like her siblings did.

"She's a chubby one, isn't she?" The grade three class crowds around, chickadees on breadcrumbs as my sister holds me swaddled in baby pink.

"Now, careful, hold her up, don't hurt her," my mother tsks.

I was always a heavy one. Baby fat.

I grow up understanding that I didn't look like other girls, other children at all. I'm the tallest in my grade until all the boys hit their growth spurts. I'm also the biggest. Even once the boys hit their growth spurts.

But within my family I am baby bird, I am frog in boiling water. I fit in until I don't. But for a while I fit in perfectly. My family is big-boned and broad-shoulder, beasts of another sort who eat their secrets with steak and potatoes every night around the dinner table. They tell me we have Viking blood. My curly hair, even with its rats nests is bestowed by Odin himself, they tell me we Jeffery's are not big, we are great.

My classmates do not see my greatness. By ten years old I start shopping in the plus size women's store, they do not carry my favourite colours. My sister stops me in the hallway and pulls my pants high over my stomach. She tells me, no one will like you if you dress like that. She rips teeth through my tangles and throws the fallen hair in the toilet, she sits on me and clips my nails and tells me no one will like you.

Women who look more like skeletons dressed as women stop my mother in the freezer aisle, faces sour and pinched and ask what she feeds me. She spits acid in their faces when they question her motherhood and we leave the grocery store. My mother is not a bad mother. When the words eat away at my skin she pinches my chubby cheeks and tells me it doesn't matter. It's all baby fat, sweetheart.

I'm ten and my dad lets me stay up past my bedtime to watch Iron Chef America with him and it's my favourite part of the day. He teaches me how to fry an egg and it becomes my favourite food. My sister breaks her yolks and tells me, you know, once you hit puberty, you'll be that fat forever. I get my period for the first time and I wish I would bleed out entirely.

The summer before high school, I teach myself to ride a bike and break my ankle crash course dieting. Two years later, my crash course avoids the cafeteria at lunch and people start looking at me like a broken bone. I flush my baby fat and wear heels to school.

My crash course is a race I don't remember beginning, there is no get-set, there is no starting line. By fifteen, I wish every day for the gunshot that signals go. By twenty, I realize there is no finish line.

My skin is white as milk and my hair falls out every time I shower. I'm pulled out of school in the eleventh grade with my face still blackened from the corner of the kitchen counter that broke my fall during another fainting spell. I start kissing boys and drinking my mother's vodka and I can wear everything I've ever dreamed of.

I graduate high school heartbroken and bleach blonde and I can take shots without even flinching. I watch the Food Network like attending church and eat pancakes every night while everyone's asleep. My sister tells me, you'll get fat if you keep eating like that.

Six months later, I'm almost hospitalized for malnourishment. On Christmas break I come home from first year university with my ribs poking through my flesh like fingers in fresh pizza dough, I can wrap my hand around the largest part of my thigh and I'm proud of this. Turkey tastes bloody on my tongue, then acidic. I give my father a mug printed with my preschool class picture for Christmas, my mother tsks and says, oh look at those baby cheeks. That baby fat.

The times my sister can sit me down long enough to speak, she asks me my weight. She multiplies it by two and tells me her own. She measures her leg next to mine, says how she could snap me like a twig. I run my hands over the fractures in my two ribs from when she did just that. Like a windstorm. I am proud of this.

Two years later and I've grown hips and womanhood. I avoid the mirrors in my bedroom and cry like my siblings did. They speak to me two times a year. My mother calls when my blood tests come through and I don't pick up the phone. I dawn a label of sickness because it's easier than disorder, than greatness. My family worries for me so I stay in my city. But I come home for Christmas break.

My father tells me I look good, like there's blood in my face, but frowns when he checks my palms to see no hemoglobin there. My mother tells me they were so worried for me, I was all skin and bones, I was so sick.

My sister grabs my leg and laughs, tells me, look at that, you're a real Jeffery now, big, fat.

I tell her baby fat.

Her nails dig into my flesh and she tells me, thunder thighs.

And I tell her alive.

Alive.

Vienna Claire Jeffery

Vienna Claire Jeffery is a slam poet, writer, and comedian from Vancouver, British Columbia as well as a Sociology student at the University of British Columbia. Writing and performing since the age of fifteen, Vienna has been a member of the Vancouver Youth Slam Poetry Team for two years, a past performer in the Canadian Festival of Spoken Word and the poet laureate of her hometown of Mission, British Columbia. Today she is a member of the UBC Slam Poetry Team, the UBC representative for the Canadian Individual Poetry Slam, and the current Vice President of the UBC Slam Poetry Club. Vienna combines poetry and comedy in her writing to share her childlike wonder of all things, advocating through both performance and page the unrestricted adoration of the mundane and familiar and the importance of loving one another endlessly and entirely. Tackling topics near and dear to her heart, such as illness, trauma, family, and love, Vienna incorporates the beautiful and the funny to reveal the bright, the romantic, the ridiculous and the lovable within every story, most especially her own.

Dear You

~Kirstina Ward

You are syllable thin. A line of worn
out paper dolls strung up on fishing line.
You swear you like the way it feels when torn
up strips of poems curl inside your spine.

You are sixteen. A whispers breadth away
from folding out into a world that will
not love you. That would rather have you stay
bent in abstract angles, trapped, until

You are significant. Despite the slant
and broken view of worth that you were taught.
No lipstick slur or perfume lie should plant
doubt inside the contours of your thoughts.

You are powerful. You are limitless.
And you were made to be courageous.

Disorder

~Kirstina Ward

Your fingers rake my ribs
back into place.
Tightening my lungs
sticky with pride.

Pull taut the skin
of collar bone and
shoulder blade.

Cut.
Trim.
With scalpel precision.

This is a mind at war.

Kirstina Ward

Kirstina Ward is 25, living in Socorro NM and working at New Mexico Tech wishing she had more time to write.

Dying to be Thin

~Tiffany Elliot

I was ten years old when, after a family gathering, I asked my mother whether I was as pretty as my cousin (who was nine months my senior). She responded, "You would be, if you lost some weight."

To see me today, you might think that I was an overweight child. In all fairness to my mother, I didn't have the willowy frame my cousin, my mother, and my youngest sister inherited from her side of the family. My bone structure is large—I'm more prone to dislocation than bone breaking—and I had just started to enter puberty. But I was by no means fat. I wore size four shorts, back when a size four equaled today's size two. I would go on to develop a classic hourglass figure, with wide hips and bust line and a smaller waist.

To my mother, however, I was fat. Within a couple months of the family gathering, she bought Herbalife pills off a radio talk show. They worked. I lost ten pounds almost overnight. They also contained ephedra, an herb with amphetamine-like effects that wouldn't be banned from supplements until 2002. I also started having heart palpitations and trouble sleeping. When my mother prepared to reorder, I told her I'd lost as much weight as I wanted to. I can still see the disappointment on her face as she set the phone receiver back in its cradle.

I would kill to have the body I had at age 16. At the time, I thought I was disgusting, but that's what happens when your entire maternal line suffers from eating disorders. (Aside: I learned later that my beautiful, skinny cousin suffered from anorexia. She was hospitalized for mono, and her doctor reportedly yelled at my aunt because the food restriction worsened her illness to such a degree that she nearly died.)

When I was 17, I finally had enough of all the teasing and comments about my arms and butt and thighs (which were *glorious,* by the way). An aunt chided me for my portions on Thanksgiving. A classmate called me a cow. A friend laughed because my butt wasn't flat enough for her flared skirt. So, I did what many insecure young women do: I began purging after every meal while simultaneously restricting my food intake. If I ate so much as a taco (which was often the entirety of my meal), I'd purge. If I was forced to have a larger meal, I'd make several trips to the restroom. I became skilled at vomiting noiselessly.

I lost five pounds, then ten, then fifteen. But even the purging wasn't enough. My thighs still met. I lost the last ten pounds by eating nothing and drinking two 2-ounce juice cups a day. At the end of the tenth day of my fast, I had finally made it. I was 120 pounds. At five foot four, I fell right in the middle of the BMI scale for my height. According to conventional wisdom, I was perfectly healthy. But at 120 pounds, my thighs were smaller around than my kneecaps. I felt weak all the time. I could vomit at the drop of a hat, and simply tasting food was enough to make me feel like I was going to be sick.

And I *was* sick. A year into my bulimia, I began to have heartburn all the time. My breath smelled terrible. I stumbled when I jogged, and sometimes while walking. I couldn't lift things that I had previously lifted without difficulty. My body was slowly breaking down.

On top of the physical issues, I was miserable. There were other horrible things in my life—flashbacks of physical abuse, my mother's alcoholism and cruelty, and the loss of my academic dreams—but at 18, I found that the eating disorder was compounding my problems. Further, I realized that I could be fat and (comparatively) happy, or I could be skinny and die.

I chose the former.

It was difficult to retrain my body. I'd been purging for so long that my body forgot how to keep food down. I'd stopped feeling the sensation of hunger months prior. To trick my body, I paired sweets and salty foods, eating a little of one after a little of the other. It was difficult. I gained back those ten pounds seemingly overnight, and then some. I topped out at 142, a few pounds over my previous high weight. I felt healthy, and in retrospect I know I looked great—even if I still panicked at the soft bulge of my thighs.

I realized this was going to be a hard road to traverse alone, so I opened up to my mother about my bulimia. I told her how hard it was to eat normally and that I needed her help. I explained my struggle to keep foods down and my new strategy for eating. After my confession, she said, "Oh, but you looked so good!"

It would be several years before I learned that she, too, suffered from bulimia.

***

It has been almost two decades since the time in my life when I embraced disordered eating. Since then, my weight has fluctuated greatly. The nightmares and night terrors I experience as a result of post-traumatic stress disorder were at their worst in my early 20s, and a psychiatrist put me on tranquilizers to help me sleep. The medication caused massive weight gain—150 pound in just over two years. I nearly doubled in size by the time I was 25.

I've been able to lose 80 pounds of the weight I gained, but I still struggle with my weight. In addition to the PTSD, I have polycystic ovarian syndrome, a disorder notorious for promoting weight gain and making weight loss difficult at best. In my early 30s, I did well by combining dietary changes with daily exercise. I woke every morning for nine months and walked through the university gym's glass doors as the sun was peeking over the horizon. I even hired a personal trainer. Unfortunately, a torn disk forced me to stop my exercise regimen until healed. A rear-end collision further complicated matters, causing the disk to herniate.

I've considered weight loss surgery and pills but decided against both. I sometimes think about the immense weight loss I experienced as a bulimic teenager. It is tempting to take my weight loss in my own hands again through severe food restriction and purging. To keep myself from going down that road, I remember how much happier I am at this point in my life and how miserable and ill I was.

I had a successful and rewarding career in mental health spanning a decade, during which I was part of the start-up team for a creative arts program that continues to serve people throughout Riverside County, California. In 2017, I left my position as administrator for a California state-wide mental health training program to attend a Master of Fine Arts program in Creative Writing, where I am the instructor of record for one class each semester. I have begun to have my poetry published after a long period of growth and development as a writer. I'm working toward a body of work and hope to get it published. I am also looking forward to graduating with my MFA and continuing my journey. Whenever the urge to purge comes over me, I look at my life and remind myself that I couldn't have accomplished any of my past achievements, or any of those to come, if I were thin and dead.

Tiffany Elliott

Tiffany Elliott was born and raised in sunny Southern CA and is currently a Master of Fine Arts in Creative Writing candidate at New Mexico State University. Her works explore issues of abuse, trauma, and how recovery and resiliency allow people to remake themselves. Her poetry has appeared in isacoustic*, MUSE, Pacific Review and Indie Blu(e)'s "We Will Not Be Silenced" anthology and is forthcoming in Riggwelter and Inlandia.

For My Grandmother

~*Piper Mullins*

the first time she ever
thought
the word
she was five,
watching her grandmother.

had only seen her hair
pulled into a tight knot.
as grandma plucked
straight pins
one by one
the girl watched wide eyed
as stark white
fell down the middle of grandma's back.

the girl had never known more than
salt and pepper gray
of middle age
colors covered in shame
or cropped short to hide waning existence –
but in one instant,
a waterfall of life
lived caring for others
flowed down the matriarch's back,
the girl understood what the word beautiful meant.

now grandma has become
shell casing.
the girl, a hollow
bullet point;

used to have definition,
but now 'beautiful'
has been fired into her brain
so many times
she's forgotten what it means.
only knows
it's *what* she's supposed to be,
no longer *who*.
just letters spelling a word
she thought she understood.

until she realized
they only meant
an aesthetic.

Poem for My Body

~Piper Mullins

when the weight
begins to fall off
you will not be the first person to notice.
people will make comments
months before you realize your pants don't fit.

you will remember
the last time you felt beautiful.
you weighed 225 pounds.

when you look at those pictures
from a few months ago
you will not recognize yourself—
you are yourself,
wearing a you costume.

once you notice,
when people say
"you've lost weight,"
it will feel like a slap in the face.
they will tell you how "healthy" you look.
you will hate them for it.

you will remember the people
who could see you back then, fondly.

you will wonder
if the ones who don't remember you
were looking through you.
you will wonder if you're losing more than weight,

and question if your stretch marks will ever go away,
or if you'll always have this evidence
of the days you were
more substantial.

You will wonder
if you will always see every imperfection through your
microscope eyes.

you will wish yourself invisible.

 when the boy you care for tells you
"your clothes are like a clown car,"
and "don't you think it's about time you get some clothes that fit"
you will not know what to do.
you have been wearing them like a costume, for years.

you question if you will ever feel beautiful again.

when you begin wearing clothes that fit,
you will wonder if you will ever feel comfortable again.
you will be painfully aware of every bulge,
every visible stretch of cellulite.

there will be days
when you will physically fight your closet.
on days when you see every
imperfection in your body,
you will want to curl up beneath the pile of clothes on the closet
floor
and hide
until you drop ten more pounds
then, remember what it took to lose the first thirty,
two weeks of illness

and a breakup that you still have not recovered from.

you will want that weight back.

when the weight finally comes off,
you will never feel small.

when the weight finally comes off,
you will feel
so small—

the first time your boyfriend tells you
he loves your body,
you won't believe him.
try to think of the way his hand fits perfectly
to your expanded hip bones.

every time you lament the fact that
your miscarriages
will prevent you from ever fitting into the jeans
you wore in high school,
no matter how much weight you lose,
try to remember that models have their hips broken
to fit into teenage girls' jeans.

realize you will never know what your body really looks like.

some days,
you will avoid the mirror like an enemy
who will swallow you.
this is wise.

when your niece tells you
that this is what women's bodies look like.

that your stretch marks
and scars
are beautiful,
"they are a visual representation
of every moment it took you to get here,"
believe her,
tell her
that her body is beautiful,
that her stretch marks
and scars are beautiful

wake up the next morning
look in the mirror,
take a deep breath
and feel free
to think about something
other than your body.

Piper Mullins

Piper Mullins was the director of the Denver Mercury Poetry Slam from 2013-2016. They were a part of the 4th place nationally ranked Denver Mercury team at the National Poetry Slam in 2015. They have worked as a teaching artist and been a featured poet in venues across the US. Their work has been featured in *La Palabra: The Word is a Woman*, and by *Swimming with Elephants publications*, among others. Piper has a BA in Writing with a Minor in Communications and a Master's of Science in Traditional Chinese Medicine. They are currently working as an artist and licensed acupuncturist in Denver, Colorado.

Everything, Gone Pear Shaped

~Megaera

I was born to a family of women, the kind of women who looked like I do now. Women with dark, curly hair that grows everywhere, even on our pear-shaped faces that echo our pear-shaped bodies. Bowling-pin genetics, my birth mother wrote, apologized for on the back of a tri-generational photograph in handwriting so shockingly similar to mine that for a moment, my teenage brain wondered if I had travelled in time to give myself some bizarre comfort. I would have given anything to have that genetic history in that photograph present as I was growing; two decades and a handful of conversations later, I can't figure out how I can say that without hurting her, so I keep my mouth shut.

I belong, genetically, to a broad lineage of women who painted, who danced, who had depression and arty obsessions like mine, with dark eyebrows and knowing smirks, who came from the Mediterranean and stuck to the mountains and the coastlines; who were, I suspect, desperate for the wilds and the endless churning sea, in equal measure. I have always wondered if the ocean soothed their hurt, quieted the rage in them. I know the rage coursed in them, flushed their cheeks and made their eyes hellfire bright, because it runs in me. I know these women listened when men told them they were damaged; listened, and died young, of heart problems.

I was born to these women, but my story isn't one of belonging. I was taken from my mother when I was a toddler; when she found me again, she listened to my father, listened and believed that I would be better off without her. Instead, I grew up under his rule, under his scarred fist. I tried to hide within myself, the only place I had, thinking, if I could just stop crying, stop my heart, just stop

stop stop, maybe this time I could disappear. Maybe I could collapse into myself.

Taken, found, and left again.

I can look at it as a parting curse, or a proverbial trail of breadcrumbs that would eventually lead me back to them, but these women and I share a genetic drift, something crooked on chromosome six. Something that makes our bodies see the proteins in grains as toxins, something that twisted our immune system to attack itself when we ate them. Gluten strips the little absorbent fibers right off our intestines, so all we get from the standard idea of food is malnutrition and pain: weak bones, razor wire pulled through our guts.

No one around me knew this, so food would be set in front of me, I would consume it, and half an hour later, my body would revolt. Racked with pain, I would throw up.

That's just the way food was.

I threw up often enough that it was something I became known for by the age of five. Enough that it become a story that was maintained as I grew into adulthood: I ate, too much, too quickly. I cried, too much, too easily.

They called me greedy, said I needed to learn self-control.

Self-discipline.

My brain began to whisper: maybe, if I was blonde, smooth, lord, if I was just smaller, no one could reach me, no one could hurt me.

I ate ice.

Dirt.

Leaves, grass, twigs, cloth, my hair, lips, fingers, anything I could find ended up in my mouth. It's a habit I still possess; in times of great stress I bite, hard, on my hands. I ate paper, with my ink-dark thoughts scribbled down, folded tightly, and chewed, chewed, chewed.

I was suicidal at eight and cutting my upper arms regularly by sixth grade.

With puberty came a terrible shift. My body thickened in ways that made no sense to me, as this body had never been mirrored before me, and I was deemed pariah, even to slap down. My father's blows came now instead on waves of sound. They shook me to the core, weakened me to the point of wishing, begging for physical pain. It was so much cleaner, easier.

How does a girl, whose world is pain, whose only knowledge of control and discipline is violence; how does she lay that control on herself?

It's simple enough: like a hurt animal lashing out against anger with rage, with more; more pain, more violence, layers and layers of it, each one a mandolin-thin slice of regained control.

Layer by layer, word by word.

I laid them out carefully, one hurt over another, interwoven, interlocked, a corset lashed with spider silk cables. With enough damage, fossilized over time, set in cold amber hatred, I made something impenetrable, unshakeable and solid.

Something that would hold me up even as it stifled me.

Impenetrable, at first to the whispers of hunger, and then, to any kindness or compliment that went contrary to the script that had been etched into my skull. Not only could I withstand the rocks, eggs, barks from the sidelines, soda bottles, fists, spit, everything that was ever flung at me, but I embraced them, incorporated them. I set them as shining jewels in my crown.

By high school, I could ignore the numbness in my fingers and my toes, the layers were so solid that I could exist on diet Dr. Pepper and cinnamon gum for days; cinnamon, because when your body is burning itself, your breath gets metallic-sweet, like rotted apples. On a bright day in August, three months after graduation and newly adult, I wrapped myself in plastic cling film and ran on the loose sand path in the dunes for seven miles.

A month later, after a week of existing, for the first few days, on a single meal-replacement drink, then half, then nothing, not even water, I failed the height-weight check for the military. The nurse must have seen my panic and smiled as she wrapped the measuring tape around my too-wide neck, too-small chest, and too soft hips. She declared me fit, within the realms of fitness entry into the military required. I was elated, but there was no water left in me to cry. I collapsed against the water fountain and drank as though it would fill me.

I was so grateful to be accepted that I ran myself broken, then ran some more. I ran right into sleeping genetics and my injuries compounded, refracted them. Grateful, until I was trapped in a military barrack, enclosed in endless white-painted brick and black buffed linoleum with nothing but time, and nothing to do but learn new ways to destroy myself.

I learned to pack my wounds with salt to make scars.

There's no memory of attaining the phone number, but I called her, my birth mother, from within that white-walled cell, and the page of my notebook that sat in front of me for that first and only phone call swirled with wild, panicked doodles and desperate notes of where I came from. A year later, when I announced my discovery and suspicion of celiac disease, my father remarked that I had been allergic to wheat as a baby.

I wish I could tell you that I have grown, Eat-Pray-Loved myself right into blissful, life-affirming health, that I let myself eat everything now, eat and dance, flirt with wild abandon and hearty, belly-shaking laughs, and paint myself, nude at three am. That I realized real love, the unfurling, unconditional kind of love, doesn't come from the shape of you, from the grace or the sway of your limbs, but from your essence, your heart to another.

I wish I could tell you that, because that's true.

It is.

I know it is, and I wish it was my story to tell right now. Instead, I have to tell you I'm still living in the middle of it, that when I hear a comment, compliment or curse, on my body, it's as though a thousand butane torches have been lit in my gut.

Instead, I have to tell you that I delight in the numbers tick, tick, ticking down, that I will take these little blue and white pills until they refuse to give them to me, and that I can't promise I won't find something else that does the same job, in a more harmful way.

Three decades of starvation and binging, the ups and the downs, have wrecked my body. I've broken bones, fainted and gone into seizures, woken up retching over a black garbage bin, braced by military nurses. I'm diabetic now; landed in the emergency room for it. There's blood in the water; my toxin-filtering organs are filled with stones and threatening to give out, yet, even as I write this, grey streaking my temples, I haven't eaten a proper meal in three days because I'm alone; there is no one to check up on me. I have deserted partners, alienated friends, torn down anything that might stand in the way of my self-destruction. I have honed my isolation, carefully crafted a reality where I don't speak about what I eat or don't eat, feel or don't feel.

Still.

I'm writing this.

I'm writing this, because despite everything, I still want to know those women. I feel them, I think I feel them, in the way I walk, but I want to know them in the way my hand glides over paper, like a gull over the sea.

They are women I should have known my whole life, but now I can only know them through myself, because they are gone. They have died of heart problems.

I am still here.

I still have a body.

Megaera

Megaera lives in Canada. She believes in the goodness of humanity and the healing power of a solid hot sauce.

G-Tube Jargon

~SethWilson I. Gray

1.

six years old sitting heartbeat
skipped outta surgery
one meal a day and puked it
skipped outta cafeteria rides
underweight sunken eyes touched chest
g-tube jargon and IV drowning death threats
best kept mid-breath beating bloodless weapons

tin lunch box creaking high school
skipped crackers crunching chin line
mother made a meal rock slide
skipped bathroom mirror glances
calorie counted hand touches were ugly
every ripple of shallowing skin was ugly
beautiful old photos where hospital beds felt like home

2.

took up cigarettes inhaled beaten stars
skipped smoke signal exhales to choke
lighters lit nail beds
skipped sentences held in throat
rather be an addict than deal with thicker thighs
rather die than feel any bigger in poison nerve endings
so starved and carved ash into lungs

nobody questions the fat kid
lunch tables are heads bent down
skipping meals makes a difference

if skin isn't falling off there is no fix
weeks eating the backside of his tongue
passed out weak fist curled around iris
hated the way a stomach can feel so full how the chest feels empty

3.

Sitting next to skeletons and elephants,
the ones we don't talk about until flesh is blush,
I use g-tube jargon to tell my story sometimes,
how I woke up in a hospital one day, starving
for a grilled cheese sandwich, the buttery crunch
still on my tongue sixteen years later.
Before the surgery, I was small.

Then I started to gain weight, tried lose it,
and that created a whole choppy vocabulary
orbiting around body and food,
a language I am still trying to understand,
make healthier. Punctuate.
Now I practice "I" statements, and notice the child
underneath the words, underneath the scar on my sternum.

SethWilson I. Gray

SethWilson Gray grew up in New Mexico and moved to Colorado Springs where he attends Colorado College, pursuing a degree in English Creative Writing with a focus in poetry. As an aspiring librarian, a former co-director of Colorado College's spoken word group SpeakEasy, and a subscriber to Poetry Magazine, he surrounds his life with the words of others because he loves them. He is published in the Pasatiempo, Leviathan Magazine, and put out his first chapbook *Thinking is just a Euphemism for Missing You* in 2018.

My Weight Problem

~Karen Garrabrant

22 lbs

I am broomstick. Wooden, numb, I sweep through extra credit hours. My emotions are dustbin. I make them small by pushing them in corners. My body strains on rugby pitch. I watch midnight from library closing shifts. I forget food. I lean into cracks of sidewalk on the way to my next obligation.

Four walls of Women's Center witness the no refuge of "you look great, Karen, like you've lost weight." I feel like shit. My tongue weakens from explaining the fucked up of that phrase, as if it were a compliment, as if it were carrot shaped reward.

In break-up, in break down, my appetite forgets itself as I try to forget myself. The depressions of my life are charted by the number of times I've heard, "you look great! Did you lose weight?"

15 lbs

We all think we are fat and we are not. We all think we are ugly when we are beautiful. I am shy, yet seek a contradiction of acceptance from any boy who will be nice. This when I am suicidal. For the first time. Pills. Cutting. Throwing up. Drinking. I pick up smoking as my bad habit. Something to do with my hands. Something to do with my mouth. Something harmful for my hands to do. Something for my mouth to do that is not for my stomach.

30 lbs

"We are not little, diminutive ladies in this family. We're not old

ladies. We're big old women. We are large and we are not ladylike,"
my grandmother, cackling.

41 lbs

My mother has ulcers. It's hard for her to swallow and she has pain
when she eats. Teams of specialists, experts, National Institutes of
Health try to figure out why she has so many symptoms, but no
disease. No diagnosis. The answer isn't cancer.

This is worse than cancer. At least cancer has protocols," my mom
says. As a survivor, she knows.

She's dropping weight at high velocity. My first visit confirms bird
bones and I take make every pre-teen hatred and fear of varicose
veins or fattening thighs.

16 lbs

A marathon runner on our track team collapses. We envied her for
the distances she spanned – the largest mileage from plate to mouth.
Her straight A's would not match the accomplishment of eating a
whole sandwich.

18 lbs

I am coming out, bursting from my shell. Being bisexual, being a
dyke, I am what early feminists and athletic departments everywhere
feared. I love punk bands. I love hard, fast sounds.

I am grunge. I wear combat boots and flannel. I shave my head. I
dye my hair colors. I am beautiful. I am more myself. Magazines
lied. They spoke bones, celery, sickness.

42 lbs

"If your mother had been a smaller person, she might not be alive now," the doctor mentions, after a stomach surgery that buys her four months of travel and normalcy before feeding tubes and a return to unsolvable mystery.

10 lbs

"Bubble butt." (No matter how scrawny I was, I always had one.)

"Leslie." (This should have been "lezzie" but kids get it wrong sometimes.)

"Frog face." (I had big blue eyes to grow into.)

"Frankenstein." (Unfortunate incident with cutting my own bangs straight across.)

27 lbs

I swim from couch to couch in a language secondary to me. My ex partner's mother palms me cash I siphon off from wheels of cheese, tomatoes, fresh bread rolls and Turkish pizza. For a living, I check coats at bars, wash dishes, and pet sit. I become the pretty skeleton key troubling door latches. I am simultaneously experiencing the euphoria of freedom and the free fall of homelessness. Isolated. Surviving. Traveling. Roaming. This shifts me more than any other experience. I am made strong by resisting suicide by thoughts of my parents and a man walking his dog. Being rootless is scarcity and opposites.

I am having the time of my life. I have never been more heartbroken. I look fantastic.

218 lbs

I am heavy with the weight of losing my mother to an undiagnosed wasting illness. It reifies my associations with thinning as unhealthy or coming from sick cultural pressures and neglected mental health. I have a few of weight loss, as others fear weight gain. I have also feared weight gain, but not in the same way. Periodically, I have associated thickness and sturdiness with strength and power. This is different from feeling fat and out of breath. I seek balance.

I remembered my grandmother's comment about being a big old woman; it gives me three goals. The first is to be bigger than my skin and effective in connecting with others. The second is to be old, that to age is a gift of more life when life is not a guarantee. To be old is an accomplishment. The third goal is to be a woman who speaks what needs to be said. To fulfill being a woman is to know how to heal myself, make the next right decision, to keep moving, shedding the weights of exterior expectations to fulfill my own balance.

Karen Garrabrant

Karen G is a decades plus poet and organizer from the Atlantic area. She co-founded Cliterati, the once a month reading at Charis Books & More, the oldest feminist bookstore in the country. She's also served Poetry Slam Inc. as a trustee, Tournament Director and slam manager. Loving poetry in all forms, she also works in a library.

Melt

~*Katrina K Guarascio*

...that this too solid flesh would melt...

Melt, flesh, melt...

Starve cheeks gaunt.
Count vertebrae poking through
an elephant's ridged back.

Stretch skin around pile of sticks.
Drape clothes on hanger hipbones.

When arms wrap around frame
say how they go right through,
corporeal diminished to ghost.

Melt, flesh, melt...

Let skin prickle with shiver,
bones clink like wind chimes.

Skirt fingers upon skeleton
exposed through dorsal skin.
Body's topography foreign
under well terrained fingers.

It's not about sexy anymore.
Not sure it ever was.

Hard to remember the initial
skipped meal of childhood,

running until knees gave to collapse,
the earliest mirror reflection that spat back.

It seems it was always this way.

Hold backbone together
with thin layers of spit and glue.
Skull bobbles on shoulder blades.

Freshman summer of thirteenth year,
a week's worth of consumption equates
to water and orange juice.

On the seventh day,
stomach heaves with the rot of bile.

At nineteen, diet consists of
coffee, ephedrine, cigarettes.

There are no more curves
to define woman over creature.
Feminine forfeits to stick figure
                                        and it isn't enough.

Melt, flesh, melt…

Keep count.
Constant comparisons:
measurements, lists, graphs,
charting roads which lead to bone yard.

Slip into winter's shade.
Shortened days make it easy to hide,
stay veiled in the dim.

There is comfort in the buried.

Secure behind barricade,
confined to bed,
no longer know hunger
or hear telephone.
Locked from the inside,
they take the hinges off the door.

Melt, flesh, melt…
Flee this corpse for better.

All I ever wanted,
all I ever wanted,

all I ever wanted,

was

      skin

          and bones.

To My Husband

~Katrina K Guarascio

We argue about food more than anything else. What we will eat, when will it be served, who will prepare it. I will never be the woman who cooks you a three course meal with bread and butter served promptly at six and sits beside you to delightfully devour every last crumb. I am content eating toast for dinner. I am content eating nothing at all. Food does not impress me, does not tempt me. It means very little.

I don't try new food. Not because I am afraid I will not like it, but because I am afraid I will and I will want more. I avoid family dinners not because of the company but the cuisine.

I don't know how to eat in front of people. I do it wrong. I eat too fast. I make a mess. You tease me and say, "I enjoy my food too much," but the truth is I just want to get the process over. I just want the eyes off me.

I have nightmares about food on my face, about not fitting into my clothes, about breaking chairs when I sit in them. You don't understand how some nights I don't want to be touched. I feel more comfortable in the shadows of our bedroom. I can break into tears when you call me beautiful.

I have panic attacks when my ring feels too tight. The ring you gave me. The ring that was too small for my finger on our wedding day. The ring you fumbled to place showing everyone my fingers were too fat to be worthy of a pretty love.

You never asked for this. I know I look like a healthy girl with a healthy appetite. The first night we spent together we ate a healthy breakfast of Huevos Rancheros without any hesitation. A healthy meal for a healthy girl not afraid to eat. What you didn't know is that it was the only meal I ate in three days.

I don't know how to make you understand. My boy with the healthy appetite for all things in life. Who eats every three hours and gets moody if he misses a meal. You see food as a show of love and care. You see it as a celebration. I see it as a weakness, a failure.

I know when I tricked you into falling in love with me, you didn't know the extent of who I am. But secrets dissipate in close proximity and I can no longer hide this from you. I wish I could. When you have lived with a secret since age eight, you learn to keep it hidden. And I do. I hide it from strangers, friends, family, co-workers, the daily acquaintances who pass through my ordinary world. It doesn't come up in conversation. I do not offer this information. But you have become something so much more. You have become precious to me. My partner. I can't hide this from you anymore and I am sorry for it. I wish you could live in the blessed ignorance of strangers but I can only be with someone for so long before my mask slips. I can't keep this from you any longer.

If you are going to stay with me, you need to know that I don't know how to grocery shop. When you say, "Get something for dinner." I don't know what you mean. When you say, "Peanut Butter and Jelly, isn't a meal," it destroys my pedagogy. I am anxious looking over menus, fearful of portion size and calorie intake. I can't pick a place to eat to save my life.

You need to know that I skip meals and lie to you about it. I neglect you to walk in circles until I reach my step goal. I believe every compliment is a well-meaning lie. You should also know that this neurosis means I still have hope. If I were to stop, that is when

I become dangerous to myself.

I have learned to live with my illness. I hope you can learn to live with it too. That you can tolerant and accept who I am. In exchange, I promise not to give up. I vow to find a common ground and a compromise. I will continue to strive for self-acceptance and confidence. But there is no guarantee.

I gift you this confession. I pledge my honesty. It is all I have. I hope it is enough.

Katrina K Guarascio

A writer and teacher living in Albuquerque, NM, Katrina K Guarascio remains an active member of the local poetry community. She has worked as an editor for various literary magazines and small presses, along with hosting poetry workshops and producing various poetry, music, and open mic performances. Along with many small press and e-zine publications, she is the author of two chapbooks of poetry, *Hazy Expressions* and *More Fire than Sun*, and three full length poetry publications with Swimming with Elephants Publications, LLC: *September, the fall of a sparrow* and *my verse*. Although her work has taken her into the realm of publishing, she continues to publish her writing under her maiden name and keep a separation between her writing and publishing endeavors.

Conversations with the Young Cashier at the Express Lane

~SaraEve Fermin

In one hand I have a pint of Ben and Jerry's
strawberry ice cream, the other, oatmeal
cookies. These are my tools, I am a fucking

artist of the ice cream sandwich. The cashier
is seventeen years old, pierced lip, heavy eyeliner,
shock of red hair.

Size 8 and heavy on a diet of self-loathing, trying
to find he self in the quiet dismissal of others.
She looks me up and down and in a half second

I see the world at seventeen again, think myself
invincible, think myself able to take without giving back,
think that I can laugh at the thought of ever letting myself

reach 250 pounds, as if I were immune
to the slow progression of time and genetics.
I knew how to fit into social norms,

how to swallow stones, how to use my body as admission
to clubs I didn't know existed yet. I was seventeen and
I was invincible, my failure to see statistics as more
than math becoming my downfall.

The cashier looks at my purchases, gives me
a slow eye roll, thinks I do not notice. I spend
most of my days grinding my teeth,
preparing for young ladies like this one.

I am a shock to their system, not afraid to admit
that I am more turned on by a ripe to bursting
sticky sweet cherry pies glossy pocket cookbook
than any half naked man flashing across Extra Magazine.

She rings up my purchases and I want to tell her to dance,
to do things now that her body will not allow
her to do when she is older.
I want to make her a badass ice cream sandwich and ask her

all the questions someone should have asked me when I was
her age: what she is reading, if the boys in her school call her a slut,
how she really feels about the teacher who is

undoing her father's abandonment
and tell her the ugly feeling in her gut is real.

But I was seventeen once, and I remember what it is like
when your head is full of paychecks,
football games and calorie counting,
exams, hiding her scale, getting to work on time.

I want to tell her I was seventeen once too. That all of the
magazine at the express checkout aisle warned me about this future.
I hope that she sees it coming better than I did.

Questions Only

~*SaraEve Fermin*

after my therapist

He asks 'How does it feel to talk about your body?'
How does it feel to open the door to gluttony?
Have you ever lived in a house made of carnival glass and
   thrown the stones anyway?
Do you feel the stones this DNA has doomed you to carry?
Are your lungs working? Can I borrow them?
What does it feel like to walk a mile in her shoes?
Who is she, the woman in the shoes you long to be?
Is it a lost cause?
What does it feel like to lose?
Have you ever felt the back of your mother's hand?
Why is your mother in all the poems?
Are the poems ever about you?
Can you ever forgive her?
Does a broken dog deserve to be kicked?
Why does it always come back to violence?
Ìs the violence related to the food?
Where was the last time you were happy?
Did you eat the whole slice of cake?
   Did you deserve it?
Will you ever forgive yourself?
   Did you deserve it?

SaraEve Fermin

SaraEve Fermin (she/her) is a performance poet and epilepsy advocate from northeast New Jersey. A 2015 Best of the Net nominee, she has performed for both local and national events, including the 2013 Women of the World Poetry Slam, the Epilepsy Foundation of Greater Los Angeles 2015 Care and Cure Benefit to End Epilepsy in Children and as a reader for Great Weather for MEDIA at the 2016 NYC Poetry Festival on Governors Island. You might have met her volunteering at various national poetry slams. A Contributing Editor for Words Dance Magazine and Book Reviewer at Swimming with Elephants Publishing, her work can be found or is forthcoming in GERM Magazine, Ink and Nebula, Rising Phoenix Press, Swimming with Elephants Light as a Feather vol. 2 and Homology Lit, among others. Her first full length poetry anthology, You Must Be This Tall to Ride, was published by Swimming with Elephants Publishing in 2016 and her follow up, View from the Top of the Ferris Wheel, was publish by Clare Songbird Publishing House in 2017. She is working on her third manuscript of poetry, Trauma Carnival. She believes in the power of foxes, hair dye and self-publishing. She loves Instagram and follows back: @SaraEve41

Unlovable

~Marni

Where to begin? I was told I was fat and put on a strict diet by my mother at age four. What does that tell you? What I heard was, "You will *never* be good enough." But I should really go back earlier, to the point at which my mother decided to have children with a man who could not have been clearer about not wanting to be a father. So what does that tell you? Every time he ignored, neglected, and flat out left me, I heard, "You're unlovable." It was said by my inner voice, my "inner mean girl" if you will, and she is still such a bitch forty-something years later. She gained strength every time my father rejected me and she called me invisible. It didn't matter that my mother kept telling me it had nothing to do with me. He just didn't want kids. Well, intent has no meaning to a child, and children will always take on the blame.

So, when does that put me for feeling like nothing? Conception? Well, great. I'm screwed. That's actually true. One of my therapists (you shouldn't be surprised that there have been several) once told me, "You learn how to be a woman from your mother and you learn how to view yourself as a woman from your father. In other words, you're totally fucked." She's not wrong. So let's think about this. What are the repercussions of feeling unlovable since being…what? Pre-verbal? Let me make a clarification. This is not feeling unloved. It's unlovable.

There's a difference.

To me, feeling unloved means there isn't anyone out there, right now, who loves you, but it will happen someday because it is possible to love you. Unlovable means that no matter how many people there are in the world, you will *never* be loved because there is nothing about you that anyone will find remotely redeeming. See how I'm screwed? It is an understatement to say being branded with that label has changed my trajectory. There I was, a child who felt unlovable, unworthy, and fat. Enter food (and later, sex).

I learned to have a profound relationship with food in preschool, when I started to realize that feelings are painful. With having no loving parent with whom to share those feelings (I had already received my parents' lecture regarding the ban on discussing/sharing/identifying feelings of any kind during orientation) I started to turn to food, which represented a lot for me. I wasn't supposed to be eating because I was fat and my mother was anorexic. I wasn't supposed to eat because my father was a highly compulsive overeater and because I looked just like him. (Really the only proof that he was my father at all.) I used food to bury my feelings and also to feed my need to rebel against what I knew at the age of four was the most neglectful home environment I could have imagined. I quickly realized what food could do for me and it was amazing… but we all know it wasn't or I wouldn't be writing about this.

Food was present. Food was comfort. Food never left. Food didn't judge. Food did exactly what it promised. Food was everything I ever wanted in a parent. Well…shit. God love her, Geneen Roth was right. Food was love (I hope some of you are old enough to get that reference. If not, look her up. She totally gets it.) Food got me through some of the worst times in my life; my parents' divorce and then their deaths nine months apart, but the fucked-up thing is the amount of self-loathing my binges would bring on. Incalculable self-laceration from which I still cannot escape. Those binges got me everything I needed and allowed me to go to my "happy place," otherwise known as shame. Goodness, I do love shame. I just let it wash over me like a warm bath. It's home. Literally. Wow, this writing thing is fucking cathartic. And so very painful.

I could not have imagined a more shameful environment in which to grow. And grow and grow. By the time I got into college, I was 215 pounds and increasing by the minute. I was already a food addict, a self-loathing addict (it's totally a thing, I swear) and I was about to add sex and love addict to the mix. It shouldn't be hard to imagine what happens when a fat, unlovable girl gets to college and moves into a co-ed dorm. You got it; the first guy that looks her way gets her. Doesn't matter who he is, or that he's a drunken stranger at a bar. He picked her out of a crowd, probably because she's chubby (she now prefers curvy) and she's a literal easy target. I am telling you it was a passing glance if it was anything at all, but 5 minutes later we were headed for my dorm.

So I had sex before I even had my first date and immediately went on a liquid diet so I could get more. Lost seventy-five pounds and became the bell of the ball. Well, in Iowa. It makes sense, right? I was raised with the idea that no one would ever, COULD ever love me. So when some stranger, any dude really, tells me I'm pretty, I'm all his. When I realized that food and sex are interchangeable addictions for obtaining and avoiding intimacy at the same fucking time, that's when my cycle of sugar and sex bingeing started. I've had people ask me why I didn't balloon up to a thousand pounds when my parents were dying and I realized it's because I was sleeping my way through my co-workers. Anytime I wasn't at the hospital for one or both parents, I was fucking. Or obsessing about fucking. And the problem with that (well one of a thousand) is that it is not easy to achieve or maintain any sense of self-worth when you're sleeping your way through men who treat you like a whore.

For my entire life, my two coping skills for everything have been food and sex. I know there are people in the world who don't believe addiction to either of these things exists. Well, fuck them all. I have gone through withdrawal from both and I am telling you it's real. I thought sugar withdrawal, with all the headaches, blurred vision, body aches, distorted thinking, depression and inability to focus was bad. But it is nothing compared to withdrawing from a person. A person! Did you know that was a thing? When the psychological pain of abandonment became so unbearable that I wanted to die. When I was text bombing him, begging him to come back to me while praying to God that he would never answer because I knew he was killing me. That's addiction. And the only thing I could do to avoid withdrawal was to use. And it worked. Until I realized it was dismantling my entire existence.

When I look back I realize what I thought was simply compulsive eating was actually a sugar addiction (Oh…so that's why I was stealing extra cartons and couldn't stop doing chocolate milk shots when I was in kindergarten. I wish I was kidding.) It's the reason I actually become a bottomless pit when I'm eating. I'm not feeding hunger at that point. I'm attempting to fill an immeasurable void and to escape. Let's put it this way, once you have the following thought you should know you're in trouble: "I can't believe I just ate an extra-large pizza all by myself. I feel so physically sick that I can't even find a comfortable position and I loathe myself to the point of being suicidal. I'm sure eating this entire carton of ice cream will make me feel better."

Sex addiction reinforced that my only worth lies in being a good lay. It's the only reason men will stay and therefore, all I have to offer. What makes me an addict is that I am forever wanting to lose myself, whether it's in another person, sex or food. I can binge on any of those things and I don't have to BE. For those precious and oh so damaging moments, I don't have to remember the shame and self-loathing that I live in and that I'll be headed for once I crash. And the best way to forget the pain of addiction is to keep using. It fucking sucks. I literally thought that feeling my feelings would *kill* me, so food and sex got me through. I thought the divorce was bad (that's when I became a two-hundred pound twelve-year-old). But watching my parents die felt *exceedingly* unbearable. Even the worst parents in the world are mourned. They are our parents after all, but I know that being an addict through all of that saved me. If not for food and sex, I may not have survived.

So when will it end? The shittiest part of this whole nightmare is that it's me abusing myself. Being totally unable to advocate for myself against me. Even when I'm trying so desperately to fend off the advances of a predator (food or dude), it's my inability to say no. To protect myself like no one ever has. To say, you don't get to treat me like shit because I am worthy of better than that. Love isn't the guy who calls me beautiful because he wants to fuck me. It's certainly not anything my inner mean girl has to say before, during or after a binge. It's not getting lost in a person, food or sex so that I can cease to exist even for a minute. Love IS my husband. A beautiful, intelligent, compassionate man, who loves every part of me, wants to be with me forever and who tells me I am not unlovable.

Perhaps someday I'll believe him.

Marni

Marni is a mother, a wife (thank goodness he stuck around), a therapist (hilarious, right?), and an educator. She has spent the best days of her life in New Mexico, so she was obviously born and raised somewhere else. She thinks life is hilarious and horrible and she is grateful for every moment. This is her first attempt at writing something anyone else might want to read so please be kind.

Twelve Steps (Nobody Talks About)

~Jennifer E. Hudgens

1. One dozen donuts, ten double cheeseburgers, an entire package of chocolate chip cookies, the empty hole inside your veins just-can't-get-enough-of a rush.

2. You've started frequenting drive-thrus in unfamiliar neighborhoods. Avoiding curious stares after the third time making rounds that day-one more hit-that's all you need to get you through 'til dinner.

3. Check the scale, 3 times a day, see if the numbers have changed. SEE IF THE NUMBERS HAVE CHANGED.

You are ugly and worthless.

You will always surrender.

4. The mirror will twist and turn your image until your hands start to tremble. You need the evacuation of self-esteem, swallowed the only deliverance you will never allow yourself.

The body never forgets,
and the demons are breeding.

5. Try to avoid your longing like the alcoholic's need for a drink. You only start to eat again, after a month of starvation-because people start asking questions.

6. You learn to hide the train wreck of your insides in between midnight binges and public restroom purges, where nobody knows your name or your face.

7. When you are accused of over eating in the presence of others, apologize, let images of how disgusting you appear to them turn you nauseas at the sight of food.

8. Remember when your daddy used to tell you, "You'd be a pretty girl if you lost some weight." If only he knew that pretty girls have a dark half, too.

9. Think of slitting your wrists when you have ingested the entire contents of your refrigerator in one sitting. The high is gone, only imagine-tomorrow is pay day.

10. Do not forget to search the porcelain god for answers, any other gods have abandoned you beneath crumbling ceilings.

11. Keep eating, until your body is tense, bursting at the seams. Try cutting the fat away with rusty razor blades-in places you will never allow any lover to see.

After all, it is your fault. You allowed yourself to get this way.

12. You thought you would be cured of the hunger when you took wrecking ball to your insides-they did not implant a fire escape in your bones.

Any Good

~Jennifer E. Hudgens

I slide my knee high boots on like I'm dressing for a salesman,
selling vacuums door-to-door,
seducing twenty something daughters,
longing to know what open road tastes like,
they try to find crumbs between his teeth.

I stretch my arms up, admiring the weight of gravity,
laugh lines, sweet cursive on plump cheeks,
baby face hides years, hides the stranger I'm not anymore,
relish in scars near ribs, scars on palms,
hair discombobulated, wrestled my crocodile fingers.

I used to think this body wasn't any good,
laugh was too loud, voice was too nasal,
sing-song melody was more scratched record than beautiful,
I used to think this body was deserving of dislocated ribs,
of boyfriends that always lie, or cheat.

I am not selling, not sold.
Not sex, not broken.
Not sex, not open for fucking.
Not sex, not waiting for white knight.

I am not a thing, not taken.
Not girl, not doll.
Not girl, not event horizon.
Not girl, not fix her.

I am woman, beautiful.
Beautiful, thunder clapped sky.

Beautiful, luminescent.
Beautiful, simply
Beautiful.

Jennifer E. Hudgens

Jennifer E. Hudgens, originally from Oklahoma. She has been previously published in Kill poet, Decomp Magazine, Pedestal Magazine, Requiem, Divine Carcass & Artistica. Jennifer has put out several chapbooks & spoken word CD's and has been featured on Indiefeed Performance poetry. Jennifer released chapbooks 1729 in 2012, For the Ghosts We Were and The Curious Lives of Harriet Turbine in 2013. She is part of Red Dirt Poetry Home for Wayward Poets in Oklahoma City, as well as other poetry readings in the OKC area. Jennifer watches the sky the way most people watch television. She has an unmatched passion for poetry and life. Her philosophy is to love hard or go home and she does so every day. She loves cheese, uke songs written out of key about vagina's, and unicorns-lots and lots of unicorns. She fears clowns, mimes, and the aisle with all of the toys that talk. She hates talking about herself in third person. She sincerely hopes you like her poems.

Heavy, Not Heavy

~Gina Marselle

I

Weight-conscious—
wore a training-bra by 10,
period by 13.
When 14, was told I looked pregnant by a family member.
When 17, a theatre director said,
        "You have such a pretty face, a gorgeous smile,
        you'd be a true beauty if you lost weight."
Never obese, just healthy my family doctor said.
A bit overweight.
Full-figured.
Voluptuous.
Never learned to enjoy my body as an adolescent—
hid inside clothes,
lost weight,
gained weight.
Ironically, the same person at size 4
as size 10.
Yet, never a true beauty to society's standards.
At size 4 reflected in the mirror is Gina at size 10,
size 12,
size 14—
I was size 14 at 14.

II

I'm more comfortable now in my 40s than in my teens.
However, when my husband holds me,
I'm fearful—

what if he finds my fullness,
my size 6 too much?
What if it disgusts him?
Even though he prefers me fuller,
it's one of the reasons he was attracted to me.
He loved me fully
when I was full with our son,
175 pounds at 8 and half months pregnant.
I was huge, gestational diabetes made sure of it.
Son is now six, and I still struggle with an ideal weight—
fluctuating between 135 and 140 pounds.
Still considered overweight.
5'2"and 135 feels comfortable. Feels comfortable at 140,
as long as I don't weigh myself. Don't obsess.
I change appointments for check-ups because I don't want to be
weighed when bloated and see 63.357 kg on the scale.
I don't want that on my chart, I don't want to see the doctor's note,
        "Overweight female presents..."
Why is this? Why are so many people fearful of a weight?
Who placed this burden on us?
Why did we never set boundaries?

III

My weight doesn't only affect me—
It's heavy when your daughter hears your
sadness over clothes looking gross—
that nothing fits.
My daughter, a beautiful dancer,
now a freshman in college.
A dancer since 2 was told the first weeks of college that she
looked too thick by a fellow dancer.
I wanted to cry.
She was hurt.

She cried. She had only heard me complain.
Now someone complained about her.
I knew how she felt. I remembered. Held her with empathetic arms.
I told her to take her beautiful ballerina self into class
and dance to make herself happy and NO ONE else.
She is a size 0, sometimes a size 1 or 2.
She is about as thick as a young cottonwood months old—
my daughter always comfortable with her body,
with her dancer body. Perfect in my eyes.
She shouldn't have been told she was thick.
Words from a bully. It still hurts.

It's shameful that other women attack other women with words:
shaming bodies—

shaming ourselves.

IV

My perfect weight is when I'm comfortable.
When I slip into a pair of jeans and feel beautiful.
Round hips. Thighs together.
In the mirror a reflection,
a selfie taken, not to post on Facebook to see how many likes—
I don't need that anymore.
I just need to feel comfortable in my own skin,
after all, it's just skin and it's meant to stretch.

Gina Marselle

Gina Marselle resides in New Mexico with her husband and children. She is a high school teacher, poet, and photographer. She volunteers at a horse rescue and hopes to adopt a horse of her own one day. She has published a number of poems and photographs in many local anthologies and has a full length published book titled, *A Fire of Prayer: A Collection of Poetry and Photography* (Swimming with Elephants Publications, 2015). Please find more information about Gina's work from her publisher at https://swimmingwithelephants.com and/or follow her on Twitter @GinaMarselle or Instagram @gigirebel.

Inadequacies

~Barnamala Roy

Mandeville Gardens.
Amidst the assembly of A-line skirts, shirts
with a common logo stitched onto the pockets
and baggy shorts introduced to shade in
bigoted stance regarding your fashion sense or
 to *enforce* discipline and homogeneity,
diversity sneaked its way in
the wide range of the shirts' whiteness-
from yellowish to bluish to camel-
the differing lengths of skirts and shorts,
but mostly in how the shape of your body
outlined by the uniform invited ridicule
or acceptance.

You had a wafer-thin figure,
"the human body has 206 bones"-
science lessons exciting our *childishness* to feel
your body to verify the accuracy of knowledge
amidst your shrill protests performed
by a hyperactivity of bony limbs.
Even behind your back, the girl
whose mother braided her hair into two thick
braids infusing in her the early sense
of the female hair as a fetish-object
chided your "broomstick strands,"
nodding her young head in disapproval

when your hair drawn back to one
thin pony tail offered glimpses of your skull.

I was indignant-
my immature senses guiding my loyalty
towards you to not entertain such scornful confidences.
Besides, I was far from perfect-
dissimilar and yet, ridiculed in no less obvious way.
The extra folds of tummy when I sat down
inspiring mock-names,
the curling of lips when the shirt button came off-
"it's a miracle they make shirts of your size"-
justifying thus the wardrobe malfunction
and downplaying my misery-
made me cover my front with the satchel
and rush home quick.
Standing in my tunic before the mirror,
I tried drawing in my tummy to *feel* thin or
skipping 50 times till my breath came out
in puffs and my two protruding front teeth
hung out as my lips parted involuntarily
 to draw in the air.

"That's what happens when you suck
your thumb for too long"-
they reproached,
our smartness was never an adequate *apology*
for my 30 kilos of *hypothyroid* plumpness
and your 17 kilos of *obstinate* skinniness,
your scanty hair and my jutting incisors.

You hit puberty late
slowed down further by a despairing aunt's

cries of apprehending infertility;
I reached it early,
bewildered by the sudden hush-hush
and hurried yanking to the bathroom
by the *tut-tutting* matron.
My crouching gait and over-frequent blinking
earned me new nicknames
from friends who *adored* me-
"Blinky" and "Bendy".
"See a psychiatrist about her stooping"-
a wise advice,
unaware that the stooping was a defence
mechanism working insidiously to ward off
 criticizing glances.

Ballyguange Place.
There were more diversities-
incurable ones, which lingered
even when you and I rectified
and grew out of
our inadequacies in the act of
growing up-
Mira's sudden sprouting of white patches
all over her brown skin
or Tridib's voice which never broke
to turn gruff like other boys
as he remained a soprano in the school choir,
aligned with us- singing better than the recently turned tenors
and yet, chased by panopticon smirks.

Then we left school, but I wonder if we can ever
leave the ghost of our ridiculed past behind.
Ripeness can only seal lips-
the speculations speak louder than voices.

But then ugliness is a challenge which
sparks your dreams and wears off you-
others hold on to it, in their minds.

Barnamala Roy

Barnamala Roy's areas of interest include researching, creative writing (prose and poetry), translating and organizing events. Her poems have been published in *Voices, The Statesman*, the South Point High School magazine, *Ascent* and a few little magazines. My translations of the works of a Bengali poet have been published in Sahitya Academy's bimonthly Journal, The Journal of the Poetry Society, museindia etc. She has also worked in the editorial panel of our self-founded magazine *Muses Mischief* and currently I am the convener of the Literary Society of our institution.

Why Me?

~Judy Mishcon

Way before I had language to express what life was like for me, I knew that I was different, and that my relationship with food was what that difference looked like. It was more than being "fatter" than the other kids. I can remember as a child standing on the corner with my brothers and friends waiting for the "Good Humor" ice cream truck that came through the neighborhood. We all chose our treats, and then I made my way to the next corner, to be there as the truck came down that block for another serving. Why me? The other kids had finished and moved on. This question was to haunt me for the next 30 years. Diets came and went, hundreds of pounds I gained and lost. At the age of 19 I became engaged, and the binging began in earnest. Desperate, I saw a diet doctor who instructed me to make myself vomit after overeating. Perhaps he hoped that this would be unpleasant enough to discourage me from binging, but for me it became a way of life.

Bulimia is a dark secret. The shame I felt about being overweight paled beside the self-loathing that followed a day spent alternately eating until I could hold no more, then literally beating myself up in an effort to get rid of the food and make room for more. I made and broke countless promises to myself about quitting, always "tomorrow". "Now" would have been impossible. I sat with others at meals thinking "just watch, and do what they do. how difficult can that be?" I was able to do that, but it didn't end there. Soon I was finding an excuse to separate myself, to succumb again to the forces that drove me to eat. There were times that my body simply would not regurgitate the food, and I would hide in my house, giving myself up to the eating. Weeks later I would emerge, having gained 30, 40, 50 pounds, ashamed to face family and friends, hating who I was.

Then finally, at age 37, I landed in treatment as a result of my abuse of alcohol and drugs. One day, they showed us a film about addiction. Up came the alcoholic in the throes of delirium tremens. Next, the junkie shooting up. In no way was I prepared for the images which followed. A young woman carrying a grocery bag unlocked the door of her apartment and entered. She began frantically digging into the bag and stuffing food into her mouth. Standing in her kitchen, coat still on, she tore into the packages of cakes and cookies and chips. Crumbs dropping from her hands, she pushed it all in, till finally she slowed, then stopped eating and went into the bathroom. Retching sounds followed; no question about what she was doing. I sat, unmoving, my heart pounding, face burning. It was me on that screen. Everyone would now know! I felt that I had been turned inside out.

Soon after that experience, I began talking in the groups about my bulimia. As a result, I went on to do long term treatment in a small facility where issues with food were addressed. Next, a 1/2-way house, followed by a 3/4-way house (yes, these do actually exist!). I began supplementing the AA meetings I was attending with BA (bulimics anonymous) and OA (overeaters anonymous) meetings. Still, I continued to struggle. No longer masked by alcohol and drugs, depression took hold. Did this rob me of my appetite? Not a chance. My body has its own peculiar alchemy, transforming every emotion to hunger. During one hospital stay for depression, I begged the psychiatrist to move me to lock-up, where eating was restricted to 3 pre-measured meals. Finally, a place to rest!

Three years into sobriety, something happened. I was at work, in and out of the lunchroom chewing on, then spitting out packets of equal (why waste time opening them?), when a feeling of utter defeat took hold of me. I reached out to a woman I had seen at meetings who seemed to have a quiet confidence and asked her for help. She introduced me to someone who became my sponsor, something like a mentor to guide me through the 12 steps. I was given a specific meal plan to follow, everything weighed and measured. As I made my way through the first couple of days, I had the sense of floating. I was doing what I knew I could not do. We spoke frequently. I felt heard, felt myself softening. Concepts I had heard over and over, like surrender, letting go, became tangible.

I had spent my life at war; with food, with my body. These were enemies to be beaten into submission. without constant vigilance I knew that control would be lost, and I would become obese. I could not fathom that the way out involved turning my attention away from the food, to allow myself to trust another person and to trust a process that was unfolding although I did not understand what would happen next. I think now that the "floating" feeling I experienced was just letting go. When I look back now at that time, I wish I could bottle that feeling and take a swig of it every time I find myself hanging on for dear life as a situation becomes more and more unworkable.

I am almost 70 years old now and have enjoyed many years free from binging and purging. I'm still a food addict though, and still have no answer to the "why me" question. That no longer seems important. Addiction is the hand I was dealt, and it has been my greatest teacher and source of strength. I grew up believing that I had to be perfect in order to be loved; a tough image to maintain when you're throwing up in gas station bathrooms and stealing candy from the supermarket. This kept me in a prison of my own making. I am flawed, and that's ok. Actually, I don't know any perfect people. We're all in this together.

I never considered my life as a gift. It felt like a daily struggle. Addiction is about survival, not living. That has changed. I have tasted life by experiencing new things, including saying honestly how I feel and what I want; by allowing myself to be vulnerable; by letting my heart be broken. As a human being, I have been given the opportunity, the privilege of feeling it all, joy and sorrow. This is my birthright and my link to all of humanity. Each moment of this stands in stark relief against the years spent in the dark. I would not change any of it.

Judy Mishcon

I am a half-century baby, born 1950 in Belle Harbor, New York. The early part of my life was devoted to the single-minded pursuit of addiction, with lots of geographic changes and various schools and jobs. Finally, in 1990 I dropped anchor permanently in Miami, Florida where I now share my (sober) life with my roommate and 5 cats, whom we happily serve.

Titles from authors in this collection by
Swimming with Elephants Publications, LLC

Wild Horses

Poetry by Courtney Butler

"Courtney A. Butler has written a book that manages to be strong and fierce while remaining innocent and full of wonder. Balancing the line between jaded adult and hopeful youth while painting the clearest picture of why the writing evokes that same sentiment- this is a fun, emotionally fulfilling collection that I will enjoy the 37th time as much as the 1st. I'll be pre-ordering her next book, as there will surely be many more."

-Wil Gibson, Author of *Quitting Smoking, Falling In and Out of Love, and Other Thoughts About Death* and *Unease at Rest*

You Must Be This Tall to Ride

Poetry by SaraEve Fermin

"So often in poetry collections, we read work that bear witness to the conflict, whether that be Poet vs. The World, Poet vs. Nature, or even Poet vs. Themselves. However, in You Must Be This Tall To Ride, we're gifted with a unique perspective – namely, what happens after the battle is fought? Contained in these pages are poems that bear witness to the afterwards; to the fighter, post-victory & battle-wearied, who must carry on with their lives, with matters of day-to-day existence. If we consider the myth of Sisyphus, cursed for eternity to push the boulder up a never-ending hill, then we must look at this work as an exploration of what may have been, had Sisyphus ever found a way to finish his task."

– William James, author, *rebel hearts & restless ghosts*

the fall of a Sparrow

Poetry by Katrina K Guarascio

"A radiant poet, Katrina K Guarascio proves in "the fall of a sparrow" that there can be something magically wonderful in words that wrap you up like your favourite sweater; there's a sort of familiarity there, but a sort of otherworldliness, too. Her writing style is purely romantic and enchanting. Laden with loss and nostalgia, heartbreak and love, comforts and tears, this particular collection holds in it four parts that seem reminiscent of a transition toward acceptance -- particularly the acceptance of falling, giving in to the inability to fly and yet, somehow, still wraps up your heart with a capability to soar."

bliss in die/unbinging the underglow

Poetry by bassam

"Bassam writes poems that feel like slow motion car crashes where, at every turn, you're also reassured that it's ok to feel like this, like even if nothing is going to be ok, there is strength to hold like a parking brake, like the axis of a planet. Bassam's words are a gut punch, a pull to beating heart chest, a hand that holds yours in the bleak. One senses that the act of poetry for Bassam is truly one of survival. What a strength it takes to show our deepest insecurities, to not ask for forgiveness. To not be the hero of your own story. Bassam is a bright non binary voice. One that asks not for acceptance, but simply is, and tells the stories of body and mind that is so intimate and accessible to those of us who endlessly battle with our shapes, our selves."

—Charlie Petch, Spoken Word Artist, Playwright, Musician

Girls Who Fell in Love with War

Poetry by Jennifer E. Hudgens

"With this collection of poetry, Jennifer E. Hudgens delves into the mess of life, dissects the carcass and sucks the meat off the bones—the meat being experience, leave the bones lying stark against the page. Each poem is both mourning and a celebration. The celebration of survival thrums in the silence. These poems will gut you and make you cry glory; have you coming back to the feast of being over and over again."

Similar to this collection

Trigger Warning: Poetry Saved My Life

Compiled and Edited by Zachary Kluckman

For decades, the coffee houses, darkly shadowed bar stools, inner city apartments, and subway stations have sounded the echo of this phrase – poetry saved my life. Poets worldwide have uttered these words to one another like a scared truth, a shared secret. Not all of them certainly, but enough. Enough to make this little tome more than a mere collection of voices, but a vital, celebratory reminder that poetry still opens the door for those whose screams are strangled by pillows. Here are the sounds of pleasure heralded against shoulders, the uplifted voices and stark tremolos of those who have survived the turmoil and trembling because they found something so deceptively simple – so heart-wrenchingly real.

About the Press

Swimming with Elephants Publications. LLC is an independent, not for profit, publishing agent focusing on supporting the working poet and non-profit organizations.

Based in Albuquerque, NM we work within our local community along with national authors to create a plethora of publications which not only promote up and coming poets, but also bring awareness to various social issues and public concerns through topical anthologies.

Although our primary goal is to create quality chapbook style publications for touring poets and performers, we also create larger poetry collections, anthologies, and commissioned publications.

We encourage our audience to seek our publications through local bookstores or purchase directly from the author/publisher; however, all of our publications are available through major distributors, such as Barnes & Nobel and Amazon.

Also available from

Swimming with Elephants Publications, LLC

the bones of this land
Kat Heatherington

Unease at Rest
Wil Gibson

A Fire of Prayer
Poetry and Photography by Gina Marselle

Some of it is Muscle
Zachary Kluckman

Provocateur
Jessica Helen Lopez

Verbrennen
Matthew Brown

my verse,
Shawna Cory & Katrina K Guarascio

Find more publications at:
swimmingwithelephants.com

Swimming with Elephants
PUBLICATIONS